Water melon

Happy B.day

...rday cake

Pear

cherry

Hand in Hand
ISBN 0-9543247-2-2

Acknowledgments: Our thanks to the staff and children of Fishergate Primary School in York who worked so hard and with such imagination to create Hand in Hand.
Once again the team at Reprotech translated the images with both care and finesse.
As ever, publishing books is as much about having enough money as it is about being creative. We are fortunate in both our landlord and our banker who have been immensely patient. Thank you Garry, Clive and Neil.

First published September 2003

Text © ENDpapers
Images © Rosey Hill
Stories © Katie Ireland
Foreword © Angela Johnson

Distributed and published by
ENDpapers, P.O. Box 69, YORK, YO1 7WZ, ENGLAND
Tel: +44 (0)1904 610676
Fax: +44 (0)1904 643049
Email: info@endpapers.co.uk
www.endpapers.co.uk

Colour reproduction by Reprotech Studios, York

Printed by Studio Print, Guisborough

HAND in HAND

an extraordinary cookbook

Sally Mowbray
Rosey Hill
Katie Ireland

FOREWORD
Angela Johnson, Head Teacher

Photos
Andrew Gaines

Text layout and design
Simon Evans

Endpapers design
Rachel Stainsby

Hand templates
Lisa Sharman

With special thanks to
The children of Fishergate Primary School, York
Bob Jackson - recipe tester, aged 11
Holly Knowles - dinosaur joke, aged 5

WATERY LANDS

🧅 **WATERY LANDS** - Did you know that there is about 1 cup of salt in every 16 cups of salt water? Did you know that the deepest ocean in the world is the Pacific? It goes down higher than Mount Everest goes up! Can you imagine what kind of world is beneath the sea?

🧅	🌾	🥛	🔪	🧤	🔥	🍲	Recipe	Section	Page
					✓	✓	Spiced Rice	Rainbow	105
✓	✓		✓	✓			Cashew Crumble	Red	13
✓			✓		✓		Water Chestnut and Bamboo Stir-Fry	Yellow	23
		✓	✓				Watercress Pâté	Pink	33
✓	✓	✓		✓			Cinnamon Cookies	Green	43

MEDITERRANEAN LANDS

⚪ **MEDITERRANEAN LANDS** - Sun, olives, sea, fruit, fish and fun, what else do you think of when you think of hot places near the sea?

🧅	🌾	🥛	🔪	🧤	🔥	🍲	Recipe	Section	Page
					✓		Tandoori (Mud) Mushrooms	Purple	55
	✓					✓	Pasta	Orange	65
		✓					Tzatziki	Blue	75
	✓	✓			✓		Crêpes	White	85
			✓			✓	Chunky Tomato Soup	Brown	95

GRASSY LANDS

🌾👑 **GRASSY LANDS** - On the plains, in the hills and mountains, by rivers and seas, there are grasses. Animals eat grasses, so do people. We also use some kinds to make shelters, rope and clothing. We can plough grasses into the soil for new plants to use their goodness as they grow.

🧅	🌾	🥛	🔪	🧤	🔥	🍲	Recipe	Section	Page
			✓				Sauerkraut	Rainbow	107
			✓			✓	Leeks	Red	15
	✓	✓			✓		Waffles	Yellow	25
				✓			Baked Potatoes	Pink	35
							Mixed Herb Salad with Fruit	Green	45

COLD CLIMATES - The coldest place in the world is Antarctica. In the year 1983 there was a recorded temperature of −89.2 degrees C, believed to be the lowest ever.

🧅	🌾	🥛	🔪	🧤	🔥	🍲	Recipe	Section	Page
	✓					✓	Porridge	Purple	51
	✓	✓	✓		✓	✓	Chowder	Orange	61
			✓			✓	Lentil Soup	Blue	71
							Bean Feast	White	81
	✓		✓				Bread Rolls	Brown	91

DESERTS - Did you know that there are hot & cold deserts in the world? The largest is a hot one in North Africa - it's called the Sahara.

🧅	🌾	🥛	🔪	🧤	🔥	🍲	Recipe	Section	Page
							Hummous	Rainbow	103
			✓				Corn and Wild Rice Muffins	Red	11
	✓				✓		Unleavened Bread – like Chupatties, and Naan	Yellow	21
	✓	✓			✓		Cactus Cakes	Pink	31
							Water	Green	41

TROPICAL LANDS - The quality of air we breathe depends on the Rain Forests. The millions of plants there release the oxygen we then breathe in. Before food, before water, we need air. Where would we be without the continuing existence of the rainforests?

🧅	🌾	🥛	🔪	🧤	🔥	🍲	Recipe	Section	Page
						✓	Black-Eyed Peas	Purple	53
			✓				Exotic Fruit Salad	Orange	63
			✓		✓		Pineapple Fritters	Blue	73
		✓	✓				Vanilla Vanilla	White	83
			✓	✓			Grilled Sweet Potatoes	Brown	93

INTRODUCTION

With Hand in Hand we set out to produce a cookbook with and for children. We also wanted to tie food into life more generally.

We wanted the book to mark out where food comes from, not particularly what country but rather what type of landscape, since landscape is still more enduring than nations.

We wanted to let the book explore how food nourishes us. For example there is a recipe devoted just to water, there are few recipes with sugar and there is a real respect for gluten, nut and dairy allergies. We also chose to follow a totally vegetarian content list in view of health and safety considerations as well as cultural ones.

We wanted to show how food is a cultural part of our lives. Cultural kitchens differ, some people eat seaweed and others eat oats. In all cultures, however, people prepare food, eat food and use food to enjoy being together. And in all cultures people have celebrated food through stories.

Working with children, both at Fishergate Primary School in York, and in the kitchens of the contributors, we were reminded over and over, through the natural anarchy of children, that food is volatile, unpredictable and always open to interpretation. Children have a refreshing logic that can re-connect us to what is sensible. I am reminded of the boy who, when asked how many Mooncakes the recipe would make, answered, "How big are your hands...?"

So with appreciation to all the children who helped us, putting their hands in the food, Hand in Hand hopefully, at least metaphorically, puts their hand in yours.

Magdalena Chávez
Originator of The Hand series

FOREWORD

Ask any parent - children love food and, all the more so, food that they have been involved in making.

In school we regularly include opportunities for cooking in the classroom. Whether in science, mathematics, geography, history, design technology, or Religious Education, cookery offers the chance to put the subject into a real life context, to make it come to life. Children see first hand the effect of heat on solids and liquids. They need to measure accurately the quantities of the different ingredients in a dish. They learn about countries and cultures around the world from the raw ingredients of traditional dishes and festival food. Individually designed healthy sandwiches are served up with pride and understanding and are eaten with relish. And to eat the product of a lesson makes the classroom a very interesting place!

We were delighted to be invited to work with the ENDpapers team on "Hand in Hand". We had lots of fun trying out the various recipes and learning about the ingredients used in the recipes in the book and the food we eat.

"Hand in Hand" invites children to dip into the pages for a little of what they fancy. Through the recipes, stories and the "titbits" of information in the book, they can learn about less common ingredients, be introduced to some new tastes, be invited to explore different cultures and try more unusual dishes. Above all they will have fun!

Angela Johnson
Head Teacher, Fishergate Primary School

Red

* Nori

* Corn & Wild rice Muffins

* Cashew Crumble

* Leeks

Mrs. Cruet despaired of her naughty twins,
Miss Pepper and **Master Salt**.
"Is it too much to ask to have you both seated at the dinner table
at the same time?"

But Miss Pepper would be in the garden making the **hedgehogs
sneeze**, and Master Salt would be **teasing the slugs**.
"No one can eat until you are both
present!"

Mrs. Cruet would holler furiously.

Miss Pepper and Master Salt are
mischievous children, but full of
character.

They can **spoil** a meal if they are allowed
to get their own way, but if they are
taken in small doses they can be
the most **charming** of dinner companions.

Nori

They catch seaweed on frames under the seas in **Japan** to make Nori and it is sold in packets of six to ten folded sheets. The sheets are thin, like paper and if toasted under the grill very lightly, they become crisp with a green fluorescent sheen. Then they can be crumbled, and you can sprinkle the pieces on **soups** or **salads**. Nori is full of the goodness of the sea, and is slightly salty. It is what is used to make **Sushi rolls**, and is the dark outside around the rice.

For the simplest rolls, lay the nori sheet flat and put cooked rice on it, enough to cover so that you can't see the nori through the rice. Then add a layer of grated carrot and a squeeze of lemon. Now, roll it up and leave it for about 20 minutes so that the nori absorbs the moisture from the filling and the roll will stay closed while you cut it into little bit-sized pieces. It is great as a starter or served with a salad.

One of the **earth's** most ancient crops, grown for over 5,000 years, rice is the principal food of the world's population. It is grown in paddy fields, constantly kept under flood until harvest.  **Rice** is regarded as good luck in many countries because people are dependent on it to survive. It has long been a symbol of happiness to come. In many cultures it is showered over newly wedded couples to wish them wealth, prosperity and a happy family in the future.

Eating rice or corn with beans results in a wholly nutritious meal because together they complete what food scientists call, **"an amino acid chain"**. That provides protein to build cells and mend wounds. It is like having two pieces of a puzzle that fit together and make a whole picture.

Corn & Wild Rice Muffins

Soak 1/2 a cup of wild rice overnight in hot water. The following day drain off the water and mix the rice with 2 cups of corn meal, a pinch of salt, and 2 teaspoons of baking powder or bicarbonate of soda. Add 2 cups of soya milk and mix, adding a little more if the mix is dry. It should be like a thick batter. Half fill oiled muffin tins and bake in a hot oven for 15 minutes or until golden. One of the reasons why it is difficult to say precisely how much liquid to add to some **grains** and **flours** is because they absorb liquids at different rates. That's why it is important to know if you are aiming for a '**dough**' or a '**batter**'. Oats for example soak up a lot of liquid; wholewheat flour soaks up more than white flour; some harvests of wild rice will absorb more water over-night than the harvests of other years. They are all different depending on the conditions they grew in.
Just like people really...

11

Next time you're ladling **honey** onto your breakfast toast, remember it was regarded as the **food of the Gods** throughout history all over the world. In **Ancient Egypt**, the furry honeybee was said to have been born of the golden tears of the **Sun God, Ra**. The bees fell to Earth, sipped the sparkling dawn dew from flowers full as goblets and turned the pure water into honey for the **Immortals**. The **Athenians** of **Ancient Greece** also knew the power of its sweetness. They promised honeycakes to a sharp-fanged **serpent** if it would stay in its cave and away from their children!

Oh Dear! The Bees are **very angry**, the Bears have stolen their **honey**...

Do you think you can help the bees find their honey again?

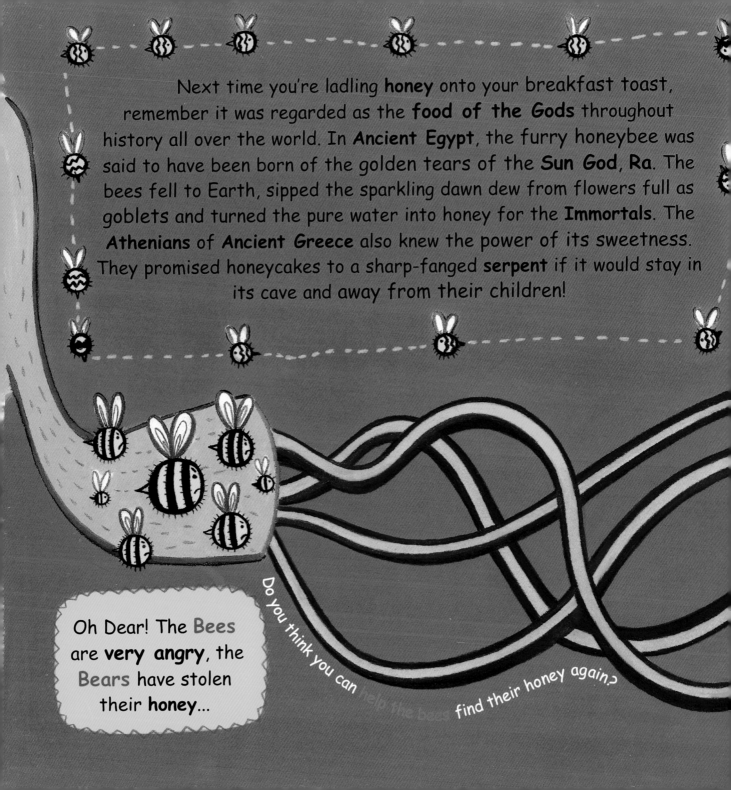

Cashew Crumble

Cashew nuts cost so much money because they only grow in pairs and they have to be harvested by hand. Imagine how long it takes to get a packet's worth!

For this recipe just use the **cashews** in the topping and make the bottom out of any **vegetables** that are in season and therefore cheaper... things like **carrots**, **onions** and **cabbage** are all good bets. Clean and chop your vegetables and put them in an oven proof dish, you will need about 4 cups of mixed vegetables altogether. Add 1 cup of **water**, 1 teaspoon of **Marmite** and 1 teaspoon of **mixed dried herbs**. Use your hands to rub together 1 cup of **flour**, 2 cups of **oats**, 1 cup of **margarine**, a pinch of **salt** and 1 cup of **cashews**. Then sprinkle this on the top of the vegetables. Bake it in a medium oven for 45 minutes. The top will be golden brown, the vegetables nicely cooked and the nuts crunchy!

The **leek** is a member of the **lily** family. In the sixteenth century it was given to drunkards to sober them up and used as a **poultice** on **snakebites**. Cooked properly, it is one of the most **delicious** vegetables and is good on its own, or added to stews and soups.

The best way to **clean** leeks is to **hold the root end** and slit the leek up the shaft to the green end carefully with a sharp knife. Then it can be washed thoroughly between all the layers and the root end **still** holds it all together.

Leeks

Because one of the difficulties of using leeks is getting rid of the mud that gets into the layers as the leek pushes up through the ground, it can take ages to wash them.

But the method opposite makes it easy...

Then chop off the root end and lay them whole in a pan and boil lightly in **water** for 10 minutes. Or, bake them in the oven in about 1 centimetre of **water** for 20 minutes.

Serve them simply with **olive oil**, **salt** and **pepper**, or use them as a pasta substitute with a favourite sauce...

15

"Yellow"

* Salt Water Taffy

* Unleavened Bread

* Water Chestnut & Bamboo Stir-fry

* Waffles

In the ancient **Middle East**, salt was very precious. It was used to preserve food as well as to flavour it. Sharing bread and salt with someone at the dinner table was a symbolic act of friendship. If you were willing to share your salt, your relationship would be a happy one. You may be worth your weight in gold, but are you worth your salt?

USING SALT

Salt is used to preserve food such as corned beef and cod. It also brings out the flavour, even of sweet things. Used in fresh vegetables like cabbage, it draws out the moisture and helps to break down the fibres. It can take away the bitter taste from vegetables like aubergine. But if it is added to soaked dried beans while they are cooking, they stay bullet hard a lot longer!

The crabs look like they are going for a **swim**... how many **red crabs** do you think are out today?

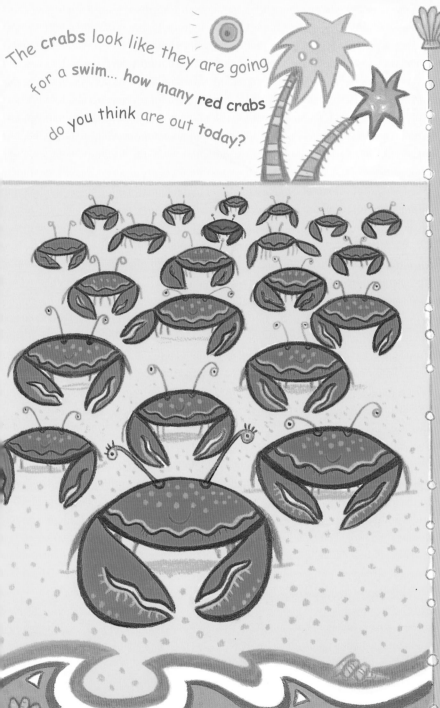

Salt Water Taffy

Put together in a pan and stir over a low heat until the sugar is dissolved, 2 cups of **sugar** and 1 cup of **syrup**, (either **corn** or **golden**), 1 and 1/2 cups of **water**, 1 and 1/2 teaspoons **salt**, 2 teaspoons **glycerine**. Test if the taffy is ready by dropping a little of the mixture into a cup of cold water. If it goes rock hard remove it from the heat and add 2 tablespoons of either **butter** or **margarine**.

Now the fun begins... Pour all the mixture onto a greased platter and let it cool until a dent is made when you press your finger on it. Gather it into a lump and pull it with your fingers. Lump it up again and pull it again. Keep going until the taffy is light and airy. Then roll it into strips and break them into bite sized pieces. Dust them with **icing sugar** to stop them sticking to each other and store them in an airtight container.

For presents or festive events, wrap them in fancy paper like toffees.

Many moons ago, there lived a **goblin**, mean as a wet summer. He would poke out his horrible pointed tongue at the hens and steal their eggs for his **omelettes**. One day the cockerel himself caught the goblin stuffing warm pink eggs into his leather pouch. He set upon him, chasing him out of the farmyard, and pecking out tufts of his greasy hair.

The goblin sat in his hovel, petrified. But his fear turned into hatred, and the hatred frosted his heart to an **icy stone**. He vowed to get his revenge on that cockerel. He sought out the red fox, and promised him one plump hen if he would scare the cockerel away for good. Then he picked the four largest foxglove flowers that he could find. "Here, you can slip these on your paws, and they will never hear you coming," the goblin hissed. But the bees had overheard this shameful plan, and one brave bee quietly crawled into each flower. When the fox reached the farmyard, they stung his paws with such ferocity that he fled in agony, kicking off his buzzing pink slippers and vowing to tear the goblin to pieces.

That miserable goblin was never seen again, but they say that you can still see his speckled fingerprints on the petals of a foxglove, and that the bees still creep inside to lay in wait, **just** in case he is hatching any more evil plans.

Unleavened Bread

Unleavened breads have no **yeast**, **baking powder** or **soda** to puff them up.

Mix a **dough** using 2 cups of wholewheat flour and 1 or 2 cups of water. The dough should not stick to the sides of the bowl. Let it rest for about an hour to let the flour absorb the water. Now knead it to release any elastic qualities in the flour.

Pull off a piece, make a ball in your hands. Flatten the ball on a **floured surface**. Peel it off. Put more flour on the surface, and flatten the other side. Take a floured rolling pin and roll the piece of dough even flatter. Peel it off and put it on a dry hot frying pan for about 1 minute, turn it over for 30 seconds. Some confident cooks puff them over direct heat. But you should follow the recipe above. Continue until you have a stack of warm breads to serve with any savoury dish.

Some of you may have seen pictures of **panda bears** gnawing lazily on sticks of bamboo. But this fast growing grass (sometimes growing as much as 30cm a day) has been vital to many peoples and tribes throughout the ages.

Only the **shoots** are eaten. The hard, fibrous stem can be used to make **paper**, **cooking utensils**, **furniture**, **rafts**, **bridges** and even **houses**. Bamboo has been made into arrowheads in times of war and pipes to play sacred music in times of **peace**. In Japan, the pine tree, the plum tree and the bamboo are thought to be the three trees of good omen.

They say that a bamboo stick thrown on the fire will scare off the scaliest demon: it lets off such a loud CRACK that no evil spirit will dare enter the house.

Water Chestnut & Bamboo Stir-Fry

Stir-fry is a really fast way to cook, but it can take ages to prepare everything! Usually people use a pan called a **wok**, but you can stir-fry in anything. The trick is to chop everything more or less the same size. Outside of **Asia** water chestnuts and bamboo shoots mostly come in tins. You need one tin of each. This part of the chopping is already done for you and it also sets the size for everything else. But you will need to chop 6 spring onions, 2 handfuls of greens, 2 carrots, 1 red pepper, 1 stalk of celery, 1 courgette, and anything else in season, taking care to choose a good mix of colours. Heat a teaspoon of oil in your pan until it is really hot,- if you flick a drop of water at the pan, it will hiss loudly when it's ready. Now dump in all the vegetables, stir and fry it until the greens have wilted. Throw on half a cup of tamari, (a **gluten free** soy sauce) or use ordinary soy sauce. Remove from the heat and eat.

23

Crunchy golden waffles
What a joy to eat
Drizzle them in syrup
For a tasty treat.

Try spicy ones with chilli
Smother them with jam
Cover them with cherry sauce
Eat with eggs and ham.

Hooray for crispy waffles
Eat waffles by the score
For breakfast, lunch and dinner
You'll always ask for more

Waffles

These **cannot** be made without an old fashioned waffle iron or a modern non-stick waffle maker (choose the modern one if you have a choice !)

Make a **batter** of 3 cups of **self-raising flour**, 1 pint of **milk**, 4 **eggs** and 1 tablespoon of **cooking oil**. Don't forget a pinch of **salt**. The batter should be stiff yet still pour.

Preheat the **waffle maker**. It is ready when a few droplets of **water** hiss and sizzle when they hit the surface. Spoon on the mix into the middle of the grid. Don't try and put on too much or it will all spill out of the sides when you put the lid down. The waffles are cooked when they are golden brown. Serve with **butter** and **maple syrup**. A good substitute for people with **gluten allergies** is to use the **buckwheat** mix for **Maple Cakes** on page 87.

Pink

* Tea

* Cactus Cakes

* Watercress Pâté

* Baked Potatoes

In Ancient China,
the art of tea-making
was as important as
painting, poetry and playing the
lute.

Green
or black Chinese
tea is taken without milk
and should be prepared to
perfection.

Beautiful, poetic books were devoted to the art of tea -making and where and when one should enjoy it. These ancient writings spoke of the perfect times to take tea...

when it is sunny
when it is cloudy
when the music is over
when thoughts are confused
when nights are long
on hot days by the lotus pond
when burning sweet incense
whilst listening to
birdsong amidst the
bamboo

Tea

Tea is a leaf.
The tea plant grows largely in hot hilly places like **India**, **Sri Lanka** and parts of **Africa**. Tea is bushy and very green. Only the newest leaves are used to make tea. Women usually gather them working across the slopes of the hills and plucking the tender shoots by hand. Then they toss them into baskets behind them, which are held steady by a head-band. The tea is then dried before being sent all over the world.

But tea can be made from many things. Easy teas to grow and make in colder rainier places are from herbs like fresh **mint** or **lemon balm**, or from flowers like **camomile**. Exotic teas can be made with the peel of **oranges** or by using hot **milk** and pouring it over **cloves**, **cinnamon** and **cardamoms**.

Pour very hot or boiling water or milk over your chosen 'tea' leaf. and let it sit and soak for about five minutes. Then pour yourself a cup. You will find one you like eventually...

Eric the turtle loved his food. He was forever being told that his eyes were too big for his stomach. One day he knew he'd eaten too much when his shell felt tight and began to creak. Resting under a tree, he spied a watermelon high in its branches. It looked so ripe and juicy. Although he was full to burst, he thought, "It's only a small one. I can fit that in". So Eric banged the tree trunk as hard as he could with his turtle snout. He was sweating by the time the watermelon finally wobbled and began to fall towards him. He licked his thin turtle lips. But, this watermelon was **very** **high** above him. As it fell, Eric watched it grow bigger... and bigger... as it got closer... and closer... Eric gave a squeak and squeezed himself into his shell just as the watermelon hit him. It exploded into a fantastic pink mush. Eric awoke two days later. To this day, Eric only eats what he can see up close. He likes to know what he's letting himself in for.

Cactus Cakes

These are simply **pancakes** made with a **batter** like **Maple Cakes** page 87 or **Waffles** page 25. But instead of dropping the batter in circles, drop the batter onto the hot pan in **oblongs** and then put drops of the mixture alongside the oblong to make **cactus** shapes. Turn them over gently like any other pancake, and serve with **syrup**.

In fact people do eat cactus - it is succulent and thirst quenching. However, cactus is not widely available in areas where it does not grow. So this recipe is included to have some fun but also to remind us that cactus is a useful and tasty part of some people's meals.

I think I'll have him for my tea

Watercress Pâté

Beat together 2 cups of **cream cheese** and a huge bunch of **watercress, chopped**. Leave it for a few hours for the flavours to mingle.

That's it!

The wonderful thing is for something so simple you can spread it on **bread** or **crackers** and even use it as a **dip** with fresh **vegetables** or **fruit**.

And the great thing about **watercress** is that it can't be anything **BUT** organic. Whenever they try to make watercress grow faster, or have bigger leaves, or be greener, it just keels over and dies.

Watercress will only grow when it is left alone to grow in its own way, at its own speed, in clear, clean water.

Good huh?

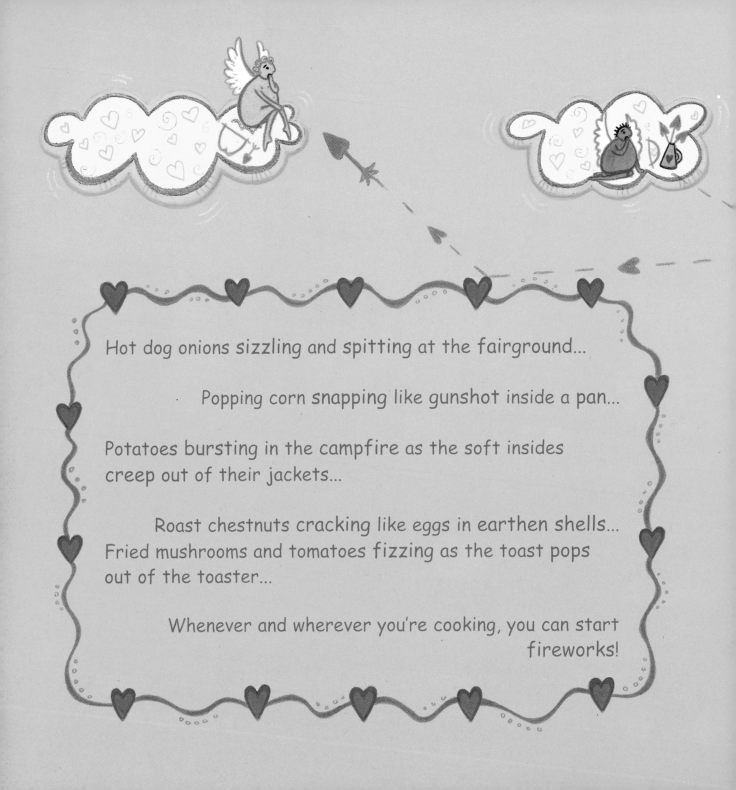

Hot dog onions sizzling and spitting at the fairground...

Popping corn snapping like gunshot inside a pan...

Potatoes bursting in the campfire as the soft insides creep out of their jackets...

Roast chestnuts cracking like eggs in earthen shells... Fried mushrooms and tomatoes fizzing as the toast pops out of the toaster...

Whenever and wherever you're cooking, you can start fireworks!

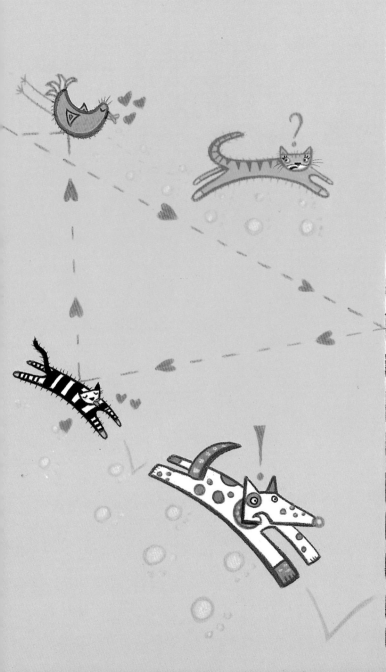

Baked Potatoes

These are so easy to make and everyone usually **loves** them because they make such good vehicles for a variety of toppings, like **butter**, **coleslaw** and **baked beans**.

Choose some big potatoes, 1 for each person, and stab them three times with a fork. Put them in a medium hot oven for an hour.

Presto!

Potatoes vary a lot in flavour and some make better baking potatoes than others. Old potatoes that are available in the **winter** are usually the **best**. And they are easy to eat anywhere - even outside by the bonfire.

And remember there are other **vegetables** that are good to bake - **marrows**, **parsnips** and **sweet potatoes**? A whole meal can be made from baking a range of vegetables and serving them just with **olive oil** and **salt**...

Green

* Banana Curry

* Water

* Cinnamon Cookies

* Mixed Herb Salad
with Fruit

"I want some
Of what they had.
Monkey hungry, My monkey tummy "Eat with us,
Monkey sad. Rumbling bad." Hungry monkey, do.
Monkey tummy So hungry monkey We never had
Rumbling bad. Follow them One as thin as you.
Monkey climb All way home Share monkey nuts
To top of tree To their den. And you will see
So hungry monkey "Greetings, monkeys. That you will grow
Far can see. Excuse me, As fat as me."
In the tree top But hungry monkey So hungry monkey
Monkey spy Desperate be." Pulled up a chair,
Four fat monkeys Big fattest monkey And learnt how good
Swinging by. Look at him. It is to share.
Big fattest monkey
See him thin.

"A **monkey** eating
a fiery banana
curry could be
called happy, but
what would you
call a **dinosaur**
who eats a
fiery curry?"

"A Megasauras!"

Banana Curry

We put this recipe in all the books in our hand series. In a way it is our 'trade-mark'. It is simple to make and it is the most unusual mix of ingredients, so everyone is always surprised that it tastes so good.

In 2 tablespoons of **sunflower** or **soya oil** fry a teaspoon each of finely grated **ginger** and **garlic**. Chop a similar amount of **onions**. When they are cooked all over and the onions have become clear, add a teaspoon of **madras curry powder** and then quickly put in six sliced **bananas**. Best to prepare these at the beginning, it takes longer than you think to peel and slice six bananas! Fry them lightly, but don't stir them too much or they will break up. Then add **coconut milk**, enough to cover the bananas. Let it boil and then remove it from the heat.

Add a pinch of **salt** and a handful of chopped fresh **coriander**.

Daisy's mother frequently warned her of the perils of the picnic: ants after the jam sponge, wasps around the juice, being mobbed by persistent **woodpigeons**. But Daisy would make her tell again and again the story of when the ladybird flew into her mouth along with a bite of cheese sandwich. Her mother protested that she had realised all too late, but remembered a peanutty taste, slightly bitter and quite **crunchy**. Daisy couldn't help but then wonder... maybe different insects would taste like all the foods she detested... beetles would taste like liquorice and spiders like sprouts... It was a theory that she never put to the test...

Water

Do you know that....

...**70%** of your body is **water?**

...when a person in London drinks a glass of water, eight people before have already drunk it?

...or that petrol in the **Arab** world is dirt cheap but **water** costs a fortune because they live in the desert?

What everyone knows to be true is that after **air**, and before **food**, we need **water**. We can live about three minutes without air, about three weeks without food, and somewhere in the middle without water.

Water can be served **cold** or **hot**, flavoured with **teas**, **coffee**, **cola** or **juice**. Fresh **juicy fruits** and fresh **vegetables** all contain lots of water. Water flushes out the impurities in our body just like it flushes out the toilets in our houses and the waste in our sewers and rivers.

Water takes care of us and we need to take care of it...

Rosie **loved** spending time with the old lady who lived next door. Lavender grew in clumps under the window and there was always the drone of bees in the air. Rosie would be given sugared almonds: **white**, pink, and lilac ones clutched in a lace handkerchief. Then she would be told to sit near the fire, even in the heat of summer. The old lady would brew a pot of leaf tea, and they would sip silently until they both reached the bottom of their cups.

Then they would **look** to see what ragged edged shape lay there: a castle, a fair lady's tear, a waning moon, a flight of starlings. Any sign would unlock a treasure chest of stories from the twinkle-eyed old lady.

She used to say that a **good story was a bridge** to take you to dreamland, and it was true - Rosie was always asleep before the end of the tale.

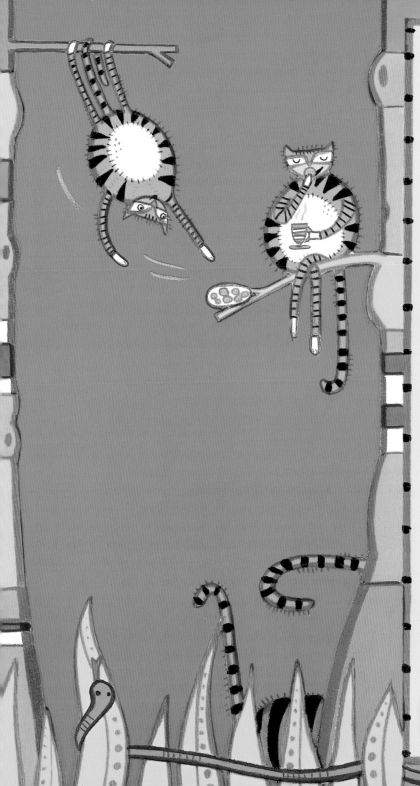

Cinnamon Cookies

In a big bowl mix together 1 cup of **margarine** and 1 and 1/2 cups of **brown sugar**. Add 4 **eggs** and 1 teaspoon of **vanilla essence**.

Then dump in 2 cups of **porridge oats**, 1 cup each of **cornflakes**, **whole wheat flour**, **raisins**, **walnuts** (if you like them), maybe the grated peel of an **orange** or a **lemon**, and 1 good tablespoon of ground **cinnamon**. Remember to add a pinch of salt when mixing the ingredients together.

Drop spoonfuls of the mixture onto an oiled baking tray and bake them in a medium oven until they are golden brown, (about 10 minutes).

Store them in a tin, if they last that long! Usually they are eaten almost **immediately**...

Garlic is something that is easy to grow. Just use a **bulb** that you might buy for cooking. Split it into the individual **cloves**.
Plant them in March about 4cm deep and 12cm apart. Just water them in dry weather and then in July or August, when the tops have gone yellow, lift them out, put them to dry and enjoy garlic all winter...

If you should decide to try growing some herbs or vegetables of your own, you could make a small **scarecrow** from some twigs and strips of foil. The fluttering silver reflecting in the sun will protect your seeds from **hungry birds**.
Tempt them with other things instead. Magpies, crows and starlings like **bacon** rind, while blackbirds and thrushes prefer sliced **apple**.

Mixed Herb Salad with fruit

It's better to make this in summer, when herbs are in **season**. Choose a selection of herbs from chives, basil, mint, parsley, rocket, coriander, and anything else that looks fresh and smells good.

Tear them up by hand. Tear up an iceberg lettuce and add it to the herbs to create bulk and offset the strong flavours of the herbs. The pale green of the iceberg lettuce will also make the darker greens of the herbs stand out. Toss all the greens together.

On the top grate apple, throw in raspberries and red currants, add a few torn up orange segments. Sprinkle with a pinch of salt and serve.

"Purple"

* Mooncakes

* Porridge

* Black-eyed
  Peas

* Tandoori
  Mushrooms

Full moon is celebrated in **China** in the **Autumn** when families gather together to feast on moon-shaped foods and remember the dead. Children dance as **lions** in lantern light. If you look hard enough you can see the seven leaping hares that live in the moon's light all laughing at the toad princess below.

Who is this princess? Well, **Chinese legend** tells

of a breathtakingly beautiful princess who wanted to live forever... but living forever always ends in trouble... for the immortal are lonely. They outlive all their friends. All of us die in the end, from a little ladybird, to an ancient oak tree, to those we love. But the princess was spoilt so she stole a magic potion of immortality and hid it in her skirts. But then she was caught and turned into a toad... to live in the dark marshes and stare at the moon forever...

Mooncakes

Still no-one really knows what's in the **moon**... is it a **man**, **cheese**, or a **fruit filling**? Put 2 tea-cups of any dried fruit in a jug and cover it with boiling water. Let it stand for about 15 minutes, drain it, cool the fruit with **cold water**, and smash it up with your hands. Then mix a paste of 4 tea-cups of self-raising flour, 1 teacup of sugar, a pinch of salt, 1 egg, 1 teacup of margarine and a cup of water, milk or soya milk. Divide it into pieces to make balls that you can roll in your hand. Make a hole in the ball with your thumb and put in some of the fruit paste. Put them on a greased baking sheet upside down and bake in a medium oven. Take them out after about 25 minutes when they are golden brown. How many does it make?

How big are your hands?

Breakfast could not start until **Grandpa** was seated and served. He took his porridge like a Scot - straight, with a pinch of salt. Silently, **Christina** would watch him in awe through her mousy curls as he swallowed every mouthful. He scraped the dish with a devout seriousness, his large, red hands rhythmically stirring. The little girl would wait until his face had disappeared behind his newspaper. Only then was it safe to tip in spoonfuls of sugar and happily tuck into her own porridge.

Porridge

Without salt, porridge is pretty tasteless. So even though people usually have it with sugar, if the oats are not cooked with a little salt, they won't taste so good.

Use 2 cups of milk or water to every cup of oats plus the pinch of salt. One cup of oats will make enough for two people. **Jumbo** oats don't soften enough when they cook, so always use **rolled** oats or '**porridge**' oats.

Cook the mix of water or milk and oats gently on a low heat until it bubbles. Remove and serve.

If the oats are left to soak overnight in water or milk, they cook very quickly. Not a bad little trick to remember for those rushed winter mornings.

51

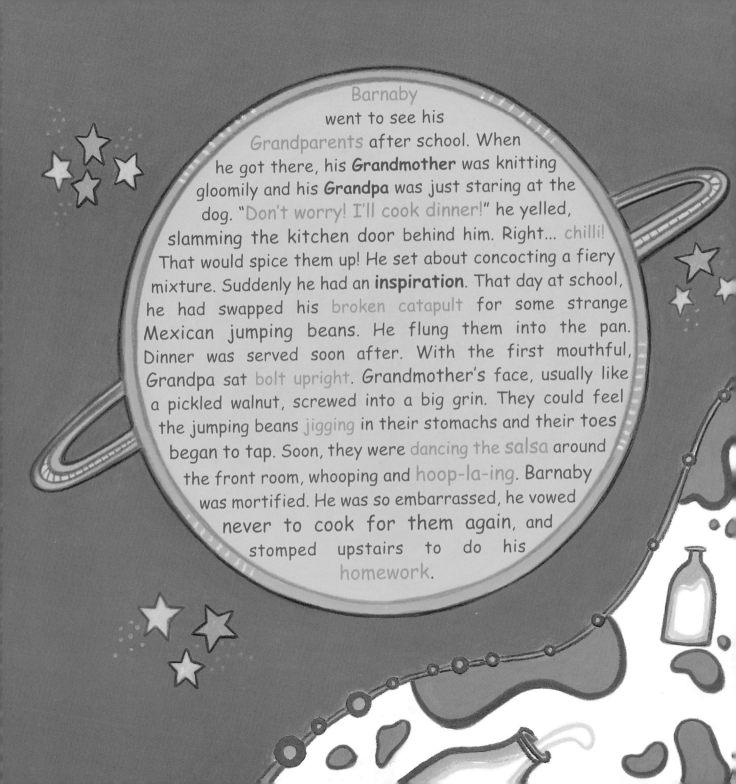

Barnaby went to see his Grandparents after school. When he got there, his **Grandmother** was knitting gloomily and his **Grandpa** was just staring at the dog. "Don't worry! I'll cook dinner!" he yelled, slamming the kitchen door behind him. Right... chilli! That would spice them up! He set about concocting a fiery mixture. Suddenly he had an **inspiration**. That day at school, he had swapped his broken catapult for some strange Mexican jumping beans. He flung them into the pan. Dinner was served soon after. With the first mouthful, Grandpa sat bolt upright. Grandmother's face, usually like a pickled walnut, screwed into a big grin. They could feel the jumping beans jigging in their stomachs and their toes began to tap. Soon, they were dancing the salsa around the front room, whooping and hoop-la-ing. Barnaby was mortified. He was so embarrassed, he vowed **never to cook for them again**, and stomped upstairs to do his homework.

Black Eyed Peas

Before slaves in the **United States** were freed in 1865 many existed on these **beans**. Today they are still eaten widely in rural parts of the **U.S.** They are exported world-wide and are sometimes called **black-eyed beans**.

They are a bit like **Jack in the Beanstalk's magic beans** because like most beans, if they are eaten with bread or rice, the combination helps keep bones strong and promotes our growth and healing. They are also pinky white with one big black spot in them, so they always look attractive and interesting on the table.

Soak 2 cups of **black eyed beans** overnight. In the morning drain off the **water** and boil them in **fresh water** until they are soft. **Don't** add salt when cooking as it slows down the process. Serve them cold in salads, or as a hot vegetable with **salt** and **pepper**. They are always a good addition to soups and stews.

The **breakfast eggs** were lined up to attention, their hats **doffed**, bowing their yolks.

But where were the toast soldiers?

They had disappeared. The last egg in line looked up. He saw one soldier dipping his toe in the peanut butter, and another one flirting with the jam.

"Captain! The soldiers have revolted!" - he cried.

"Just see what they are doing!"

The Captain frowned as a soldier went by, hand in hand with the ketchup.

"They will be back," - he replied.

"People may enjoy bread with jam, bread with peanut butter, even..."

- he pulled a face -

"... **ketchup sandwiches**, but boiled eggs and soldiers will always be the best. Our time will come again."

And he returned to the barracks to report to the **bacon**...

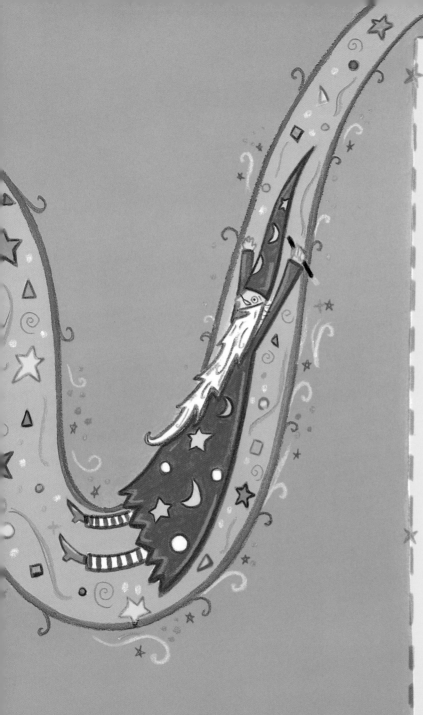

Tandoori (Mud) Mushrooms

Tandoori, or Mud, Mushrooms are easy to make, just sweat out the **natural water** in the **mushrooms** like this: cover the bottom of a big pan or wok with **sunflower oil** and heat it gently.

By the time you have rinsed 6 **mushrooms** for each person you want to feed, the **oil** will be hot enough for you to put the mushrooms in. Turn up the heat and add 1 teaspoon of **tandoori spice** and a pinch of **salt** for every 12 mushrooms. Keep moving the mushrooms around so none of them are left on the base of the pan to over-cook.

The **salt** and the **spice** will draw out the juices of the mushrooms resulting in a thick mud-like sauce as they cook.

Delicious!

Orange

* Tapanade

* Chowder

* Exotic Fruit
  Salad

* Pasta

Legend
tells us that coffee was discovered by an Arabian monk in the twelfth century.

One day he was watching the goats grazing on fruits and leaves on the hillside. When they suddenly began to **gambol** and **frolic** excitedly, rushing amongst the bushes, he went to investigate, and found the coffee tree. It was covered in clusters of white flowers and little shiny red berries.

He took some of these berries and brewed up an **infusion** for the other monks. They took four sips each to keep them awake during their long evening meditations... but we need to be careful what beans and seeds we pick and brew up. Some could have the opposite effect and make us sleep forever...

Tapanade

Tapanade is simply a paste made from crushed olives, crushed so finely that it can be spread on bread... Choose black or green olives and make sure they don't have any stones in them. Put a tea-cup full in a bowl and add about half a cup of olive oil. Use a potato masher or an electric blender and whizz it up.

Olives are salty so you don't need to add salt, but you can add a pinch of chilli or garlic, maybe a squeeze of lemon juice or herbs like thyme or oregano.

Smell and see which of these appeals to you... although it is probably a good idea not to add them all together!

59

The cactus, or prickly pear, has evolved to survive the low rainfall and drought of the **desert**. Many species have developed very long and heavy tendril roots that seek out moisture from far below through cracks in the rocks. One cactus is called "Queen of the Night", and bears **luminous blossoms** that only come out in moonlight and give off a heady, musky perfume.

Others, like the "Strawberry Hedgehog" cactus, collect condensation on their prickles so their roots can drink it up when it drips onto the ground. Birds nest in the prickles, in the hope that the sharp needles will protect their young from animals that might attack.

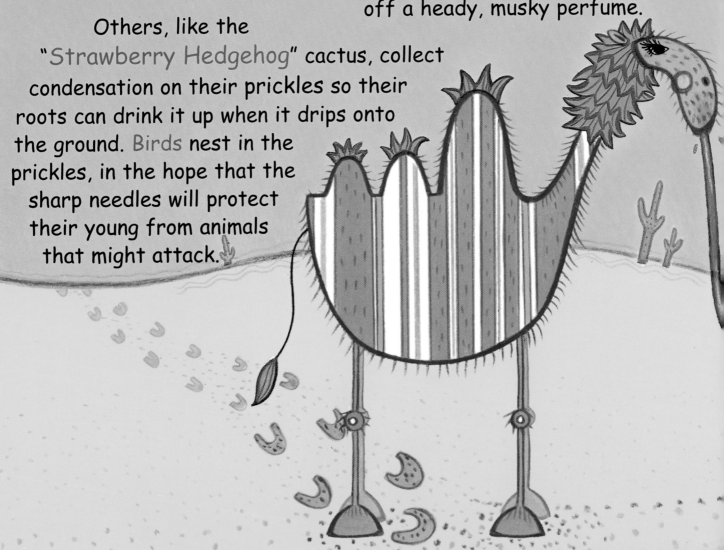

Chowder

This is a fancy name for a thick **soup**. And this one is made in two parts.

First, chop into cubes 3 big potatoes and boil until soft in 2 pints of water, with a pinch of salt, and either 4 fresh sage leaves, or a teaspoon of dried sage.

Then, in another pan, fry gently a chopped onion in 3 tablespoons of butter or margarine . When the onion is translucent or clear, remove from the heat and make a paste by stirring in 3 tablespoons of whole wheat flour. Return to the heat and gently stir in the water, sage and potatoes. Stir on a gentle heat until the chowder thickens.

Add sweet corn or diced spring onions for colour and flavour. Add more salt if it needs it, top with grated cheese and serve.

61

Exotic Fruit Salad

An outdoor **market** is a great place to go to choose what is needed. Be sure to look for things like **papaya**, **mangoes**, **pineapples**, **kiwi fruits**, **lychees**, to create something really **exotic**. Prepare all the fruits by washing them first and checking which need to be peeled. Ask if you are not sure - **mangoes** need peeling, so do **lychees** and **papaya**. **Pineapples** need more than peeling, they need really heavy work when they are tough and scaly. Some fruits, like mangoes, have HUGE stones, others, like kiwi fruits have seeds that are easily eaten. Cut them into chunky pieces and mix together.

Go for **colour** and quality always, and remember that what is exotic to one person is ordinary to another. What do you think is the most exotic fruit in **Sri Lanka** for example? An apple - because they don't grow there...

63

When
Thomas
found a monster
Crouched under the
kitchen sink,
He shooed him away -
"Go home, I say
What will my mother think?"

"But I'm enjoying your mother's
pasta -
It's very good in fact.
Full of carbohydrates
And things we monsters lack."

"But that bowl is full of
worms and string!
That's not my mother's cooking!
How can you eat that awful stuff?
It's all brown and wriggling!"

The monster sighed and rolled his eyes.
"Well, it's pasta in my opinion."

See, if you know things by their proper names,
You know just what you're eating.
Listen to a wise old monster.
And learn a little something -
In Italian:
Vermicelli means 'little worms'
And spaghetti, 'little string.'

Pasta

Pasta is made from **flour** and **water**, pressed into shapes and left to dry.

The fresh pasta that can be bought is pasta before it is dried which is why it is wet and slippery. Sometimes pasta is made from things like **rice** and **corn** but usually it is made from **wheat**.

Boil 2 cups of pasta in 4 cups of water for about 20 minutes, to feed 2 hungry people. Drain and serve with toppings.

Fresh grated **tomatoes** with torn up basil leaves and **cracked pepper** is good. Or, add grated **cheese** and watch it melt. Alternatively just pasta with **olive oil**, **salt** and **pepper** is great!

Blue

* Guacamole

* Lentil Soup

* Pineapple Fritters

* Tzatziki

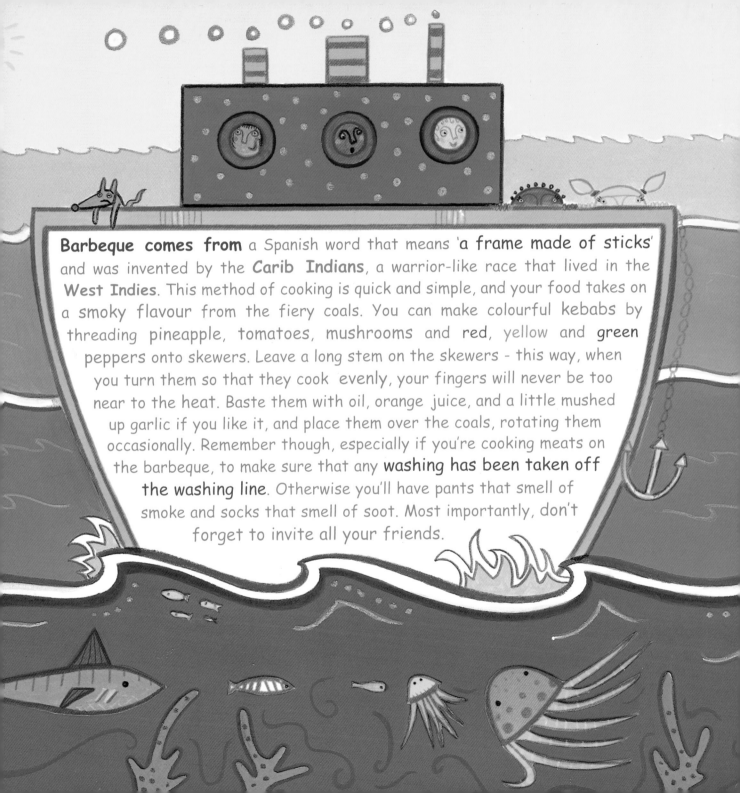

Barbeque comes from a Spanish word that means 'a frame made of sticks' and was invented by the **Carib Indians**, a warrior-like race that lived in the **West Indies**. This method of cooking is quick and simple, and your food takes on a smoky flavour from the fiery coals. You can make colourful kebabs by threading pineapple, tomatoes, mushrooms and red, yellow and green peppers onto skewers. Leave a long stem on the skewers - this way, when you turn them so that they cook evenly, your fingers will never be too near to the heat. Baste them with oil, orange juice, and a little mushed up garlic if you like it, and place them over the coals, rotating them occasionally. Remember though, especially if you're cooking meats on the barbeque, to make sure that any **washing has been taken off the washing line**. Otherwise you'll have pants that smell of smoke and socks that smell of soot. Most importantly, don't forget to invite all your friends.

Guacamole

This is a **Mexican** favourite for dipping **tortilla** chips and is just as good on **bread** or **toast**. Don't make **guacamole** too far in advance as **avocadoes,** just like apples, go brown very quickly once they have been peeled.

Choose avocados that are soft, so that when you press them you can see your finger print on them. One avocado will make enough guacamole for about eight slices of bread. You can always make it go further by adding some plain yoghourt or soured cream. Peel off the outside of the avocado, squeeze it open, and throw away the stone. Use a spoon to get as much of the pulp away from the skin as possible. Mash the pulp with a fork and add a pinch of salt, a teaspoon of lemon juice and some black pepper.

Adding chopped tomatoes or spring onions requires a knife but is also tasty...

69

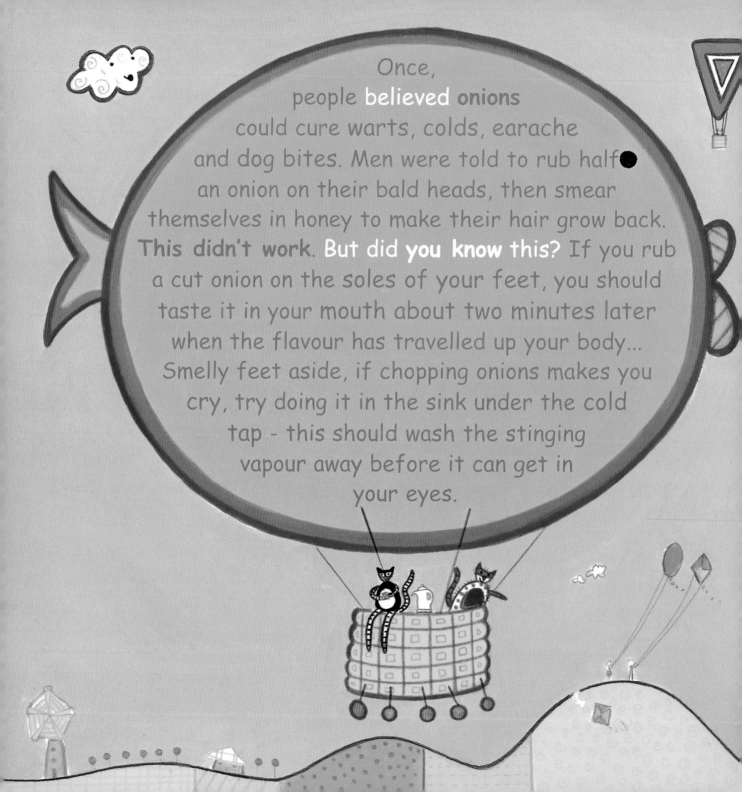

Once,
people **believed onions**
could cure warts, colds, earache
and dog bites. Men were told to rub half
an onion on their bald heads, then smear
themselves in honey to make their hair grow back.
This didn't work. But did **you know** this? If you rub
a cut onion on the soles of your feet, you should
taste it in your mouth about two minutes later
when the flavour has travelled up your body...
Smelly feet aside, if chopping onions makes you
cry, try doing it in the sink under the cold
tap - this should wash the stinging
vapour away before it can get in
your eyes.

Lentil Soup

It is the simplest of soups and yet the king and queen of soups. Nothing is quite so hearty and so flavourful, all by itself, as **lentil soup**.

The more **lentils** the thicker the soup. Use **split red lentils**, which aren't red at all but bright orange.

It is possible to make a soup with just lentils and **salt**. But this one has a little **oil**, some **herbs** and an **onion** too.

Grate an **onion** into a pan with 1 tablespoon of **cooking oil**. Let it fry gently. Add a teaspoon of **mixed dried herbs**, 1 cup of **red lentils** and 3 cups of **water**. Let it simmer (boil gently) until the lentils have disappeared and become an orange mash. Add a bit of **salt** (or **Marmite** is good) and **fresh herbs** to garnish are always fun.

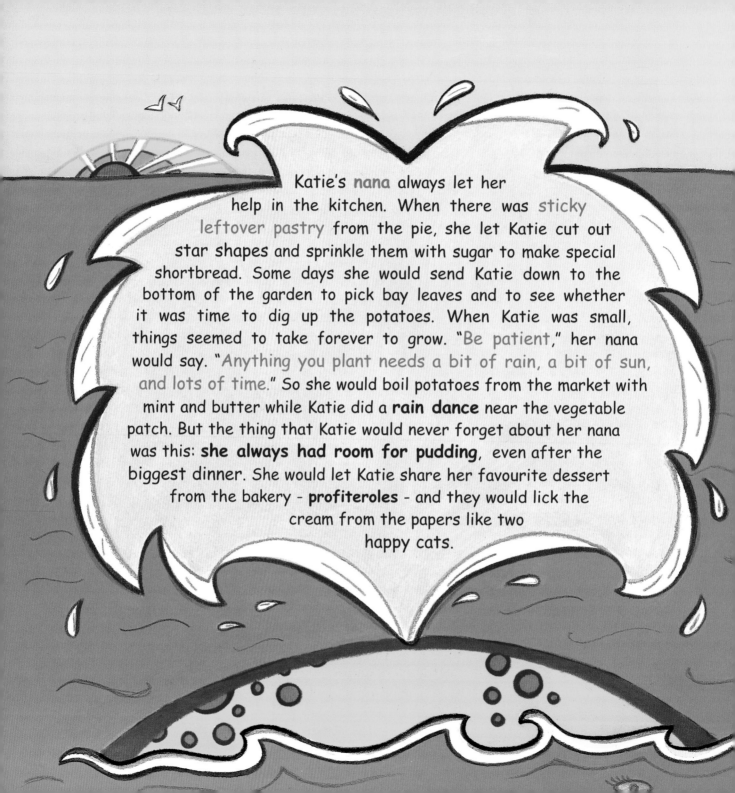

Katie's **nana** always let her help in the kitchen. When there was sticky leftover pastry from the pie, she let Katie cut out star shapes and sprinkle them with sugar to make special shortbread. Some days she would send Katie down to the bottom of the garden to pick bay leaves and to see whether it was time to dig up the potatoes. When Katie was small, things seemed to take forever to grow. "Be patient," her nana would say. "Anything you plant needs a bit of rain, a bit of sun, and lots of time." So she would boil potatoes from the market with mint and butter while Katie did a **rain dance** near the vegetable patch. But the thing that Katie would never forget about her nana was this: **she always had room for pudding**, even after the biggest dinner. She would let Katie share her favourite dessert from the bakery - **profiteroles** - and they would lick the cream from the papers like two happy cats.

Pineapple Fritters

Test the **pineapple** by pulling one of the inner **leaves**. If it comes out easily the fruit is ripe.

Cut off the top and the bottom of the pineapple **BEFORE** trying to cut the sides. It will give a strong flat base to put on the chopping surface so you can cut off the sides by pushing down with the knife from top to bottom. Work your way round the pineapple... don't worry about the '**eyes**', the black dots which are still in the fruit. You can gouge them out with a knife or a potato peeler, but no-one will notice if you don't.

Once you have cut the pineapple into bite sized chunks, dip them in a batter of 1 cup of chick pea flour (gram flour) and 1 cup of water, and then fry them in hot cooking oil until they are golden. After you have smothered your warm pinapple fritters with honey or syrup, no one will be looking to see if the eyes are still there...

The peacocks were the most beautiful creatures that the baby orang-utans had ever seen. They shimmered in and out of the sunlit leaf-shadow as graceful as fish underwater. Their feathers were the inkiest blues of the heavens and the pearliest greens of the oceans. But they teased the baby orang-utans.

"You will never be as magnificent as us," the peacocks would crow. The baby orang-utans knew the peacocks were right. They only had to look at their elders to know that. Old Grandfather Orang-utan saw how this made the babies sad. He loped over.

"Everyone knows that what is outside may disguise what is inside." And with that, he sprang up the nearest tree. In the flash of a hummingbird's wings he was back. For one so old, he moved fast. Grandfather Orang-utan held up a coconut.

"Look how brown and hairy this coconut is on the outside -just like you", he laughed, poking one of them in the tummy. They all giggled. He smashed the coconut on a mossy rock. "But inside there's pure white flesh to chew on and enough milk for everyone."

So the baby orang-utans sat in the sun, happily munching on coconut and drinking its sweet milk, as they watched the peacocks walk by.

Tzatziki

This is based on a **Greek** dish and is great for spreading on **breads** or **pancakes**, serving with **salads** and using as a dip for raw **vegetables**.

Choose a large carton, 500g, of plain thick yoghurt and mix it with 1 clove of grated garlic, either a teaspoon of dried mint or ideally six fresh mint leaves, torn up into small pieces, and 1 grated cucumber.

However, without this next little trick the yoghurt will soon become watery and thin... The trick is to squeeze all the cucumber juice out of the cucumber after it is grated and before adding it to the yoghurt.

Delicious!

White

* Coffee

* Bean Feast

* Vanilla Vanilla

* Crêpes

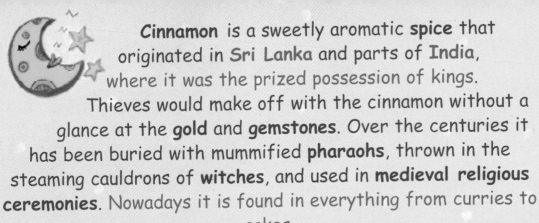

Cinnamon is a sweetly aromatic **spice** that originated in **Sri Lanka** and parts of **India**, where it was the prized possession of kings. Thieves would make off with the cinnamon without a glance at the **gold** and **gemstones**. Over the centuries it has been buried with mummified **pharaohs**, thrown in the steaming cauldrons of **witches**, and used in **medieval religious ceremonies**. Nowadays it is found in everything from curries to cakes.

It is especially popular at festive times, when its warm scent **mingles** with other traditional scents of orange, clove and bruised pine needles. You can even hang bundles of cinnamon sticks on your **Christmas tree**...

Coffee

Coffee is made from beans that are just like baked beans or peanuts, (lots of people don't know that peanuts are **not** nuts at all...)

The beans are **roasted** which gives them that special 'coffee' flavour. To make this simple drink, grind the beans up to release all the flavour kept inside. Then **infuse** in hot **water**, and see the clear liquid turn into coffee before your very eyes. '**Infuse**' is used to describe how the ground coffee or 'grinds' are allowed to float to the top and then sink in their own time through the hot water.

Put 1 tablespoon of **ground coffee** per person in a litre plastic jug. For each person add half a litre of **boiling water.**

Wait. Stir.

When most of the grounds have fallen to the bottom either gently pour the liquid into a cup or sieve through a tea-strainer. Strong, **frothy** and no bitterness...

It's commonly thought
  That mice prefer cheese
    Rabbits like carrots
      And penguins want seeds.
But what a dull place this world would be
If we couldn't choose what we liked for tea.

  So next time your dog
    Begs for a treat,
      Think of something new
        He might like to eat.
      Nothing too sweet,
        Nothing too rich,
          But perhaps he'd love
            A pickle sandwich?

Bean Feast

There are so many tinned beans to buy these days that a **bean feast** can be made very quickly, needs no cooking, just a skill with the tin opener...

This feast can also be made from dried beans that are much cheaper. Planning ahead is essential as dried beans take a long time to prepare. First they need soaking overnight, which is great fun since they DOUBLE in size, and then they need boiling for a long time until they are soft.

Choose the beans for colour, chick peas are light brown, kidney beans red, black beans black, cannellini beans white, broad beans green. A nice mix looks very appetising. Tear up fresh parsley and scatter over the top with a dash of salt.

Vanilla pods are the fruits of a tropical creeping orchid found in **Mexico** and **Madagascar**, which winds round trees and clings to rocks. Each of the **stunning white flowers** only blooms for **one** day and can only be pollinated by one particular sort of small **special bee**. When the golden green pods are picked they are laid out to roast in the hot sun for ten days until they turn a **chocolaty brown**.

Vanilla Vanilla

This is made with a vanilla **cream**, vanilla **baked oats** and vanilla, **sugar**. Perhaps it should be called vanilla vanilla **vanilla**?

Put some **sugar** in a clean covered jam jar with a **vanilla pod** for about a week.

In a bowl mix 1 cup of **oats**, 1 cup of grated **bread crumbs** with 1 cup of **pecans** or **walnuts** and 1/2 a cup of **sugar**. Finally, add 1 teaspoon of **vanilla essence** and toss the mixture around in the bowl. Spread it on a baking sheet and roast in a medium oven for 10 minutes, until **crunchy**.

In a separate bowl beat 2 cups of **cream** until it is stiff, using an **electric beater** or an **egg beater**. A fork or whisk will take a long time and makes arms very tired. Add 1/2 a cup **brown sugar** and 1 teaspoon of **vanilla essence** and a pinch of **salt**. Fold in the bread and oats. Refrigerate for an hour, serve topped with some of the vanilla sugar.

Jean-Paul the pot-bellied pig had a busy day ahead. He was preparing a surprise birthday party for his dear friend, François. He nearly tripped over his trotters as he clattered downstairs to the kitchen. He set about mixing creamy crêpe batter, then swirling... flipping... swirling... flipping... until he had a tall, teetering pile of hot, steaming crêpes. One pile was layered with jambon and brie, the other was dripping with bananas and cream. He huffed as he struggled with his jacket and puffed as he dashed out the door, juggling the two crêpe towers. Once in the forest, he shook out his picnic blanket and waited for François. When the astonished little pig got there, the nightingales were singing Happy Birthday, the glow-worms were lighting up the trees and the butterflies were floating down from the branches like confetti. And you can bet that the two little pigs ate every last bit of those two tall teetering piles of hot steamy crêpes.

Crêpes

These are very thin **pancakes**, but they have a lot of **eggs** in them which make them strong. Mix 2 heaped tablespoons of wholewheat flour with 2 cups of milk and 4 eggs. In a non-stick frying pan, melt less than a teaspoon of butter, by turning the pan to just above half-heat. When the **butter** has melted, spoon in about 2 or 3 tablespoons of the mixture. With the handle of the pan, tip it so the base is covered with mixture. As the edges dry and the pancake looses its shine, loosen it with a plastic spatula and turn it.

The first **crêpes** are often thick and tricky but keep going. As the next ones are cooked there will be improvement - don't ask why, it's part of the magic of cooking... Eat with sugar and lemon or fill them with sautéed mushrooms, salad or anything else you fancy. As you get better at making them, and they get thinner and thinner, you'll get more and more out...

"Brown"

* Maple Cakes

* Bread Rolls

* Grilled Sweet
    Potatoes

* Chunky Tomato
    Soup

There's no fun like bobbing for
apples,
So take a deep breath and duck.
It's always the one with the big
mouth
Who has all the bobbing luck.

But apples can be rather hard–
I remember one Halloween
Complications with Grandma's
dentures,
So now we use nectarines.

Maple Cakes

Maple syrup is the sap of Maple trees and tastes sweet like cinder caramel. And **buckwheat** is not wheat at all but the triangular prism seeds of a herb...

Mix a **batter** using a cup of **buckwheat flour**, 3 cups of **warm**, not hot, **water**, a pinch of **salt** and a teaspoon of **yeast**. Leave that to one side for about an hour and then heat a frying pan, griddle or flat hot plate. Test the heat of the pan / plate by wetting your fingers and throwing a few sprinkles of water onto it. If it goes 'hiss' it's ready. Drop the batter in tablespoon fulls to make circles on the pan / plate. Turn the cakes over and cook them on the other side. Only turn them when they are drying around the edges and the bubbles forming in the batter pop and leave small craters. They need less time to cook on the second side. You can always check and see if they are done enough. Then serve them with **maple syrup**.

89

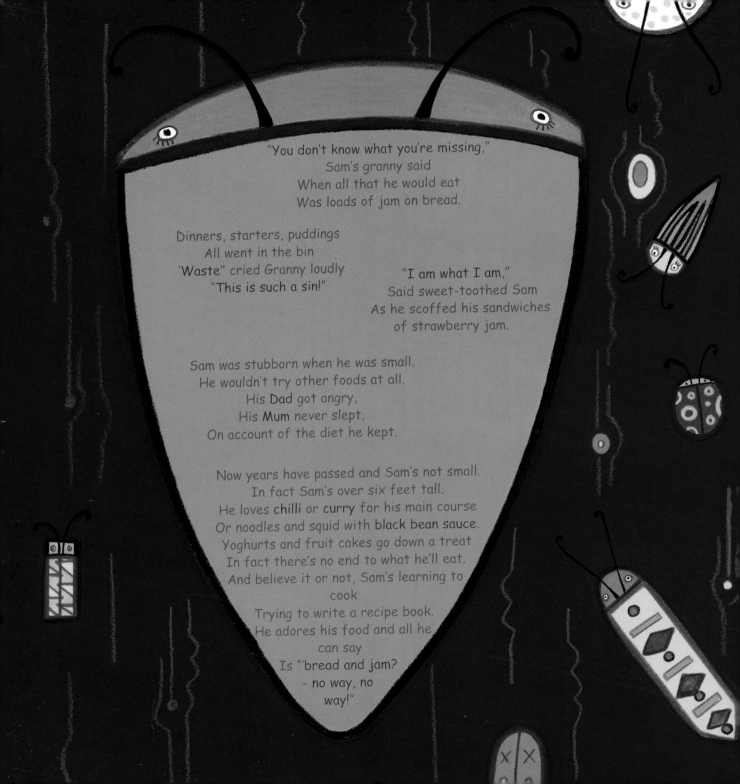

"You don't know what you're missing,"
Sam's granny said
When all that he would eat
Was loads of jam on bread.

Dinners, starters, puddings
All went in the bin
'Waste" cried Granny loudly
"This is such a sin!"

"I am what I am,"
Said sweet-toothed Sam
As he scoffed his sandwiches
of strawberry jam.

Sam was stubborn when he was small.
He wouldn't try other foods at all.
His Dad got angry,
His Mum never slept,
On account of the diet he kept.

Now years have passed and Sam's not small.
In fact Sam's over six feet tall.
He loves chilli or curry for his main course
Or noodles and squid with black bean sauce.
Yoghurts and fruit cakes go down a treat
In fact there's no end to what he'll eat.
And believe it or not, Sam's learning to
cook
Trying to write a recipe book.
He adores his food and all he
can say
Is "'bread and jam?
- no way, no
way!"

Bread Rolls

Mix together 1 Kg of **whole-wheat flour** with 2 tablespoons of dried **yeast** and 2 tablespoons of **sugar**. Yeast likes to eat sugar and the sugar helps it grow which makes the bread rise. Yeast hates salt. **Salt** kills it. So when the pinch of **salt** goes in, make sure it DOESN'T go right on top of the yeast!

Now add warm **water**, about as hot as your hands, maybe a bit warmer. If the water is too hot or too cold it will also kill the yeast... add water to make a dough. (wet enough to be sticky but dry enough to clean the sides of the bowl)

Form the dough into rolls - they can be any shape. Leave them on an oiled baking tray to rise for about 10 minutes. Cover the tray with a towel to keep them warm. They are ready when you push gently with your finger and the dough springs back. Bake in a hot oven for 10 minutes or until they are golden.

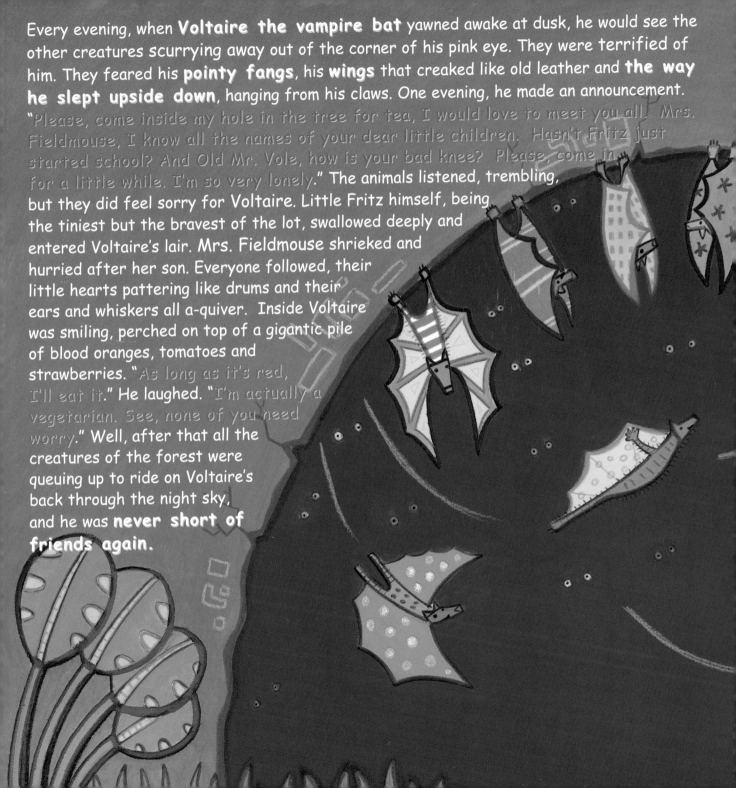

Every evening, when **Voltaire the vampire bat** yawned awake at dusk, he would see the other creatures scurrying away out of the corner of his pink eye. They were terrified of him. They feared his **pointy fangs**, his **wings** that creaked like old leather and **the way he slept upside down**, hanging from his claws. One evening, he made an announcement. "Please, come inside my hole in the tree for tea, I would love to meet you all. Mrs. Fieldmouse, I know all the names of your dear little children. Hasn't Fritz just started school? And Old Mr. Vole, how is your bad knee? Please, come in for a little while. I'm so very lonely." The animals listened, trembling, but they did feel sorry for Voltaire. Little Fritz himself, being the tiniest but the bravest of the lot, swallowed deeply and entered Voltaire's lair. Mrs. Fieldmouse shrieked and hurried after her son. Everyone followed, their little hearts pattering like drums and their ears and whiskers all a-quiver. Inside Voltaire was smiling, perched on top of a gigantic pile of blood oranges, tomatoes and strawberries. "As long as it's red, I'll eat it." He laughed. "I'm actually a vegetarian. See, none of you need worry." Well, after that all the creatures of the forest were queuing up to ride on Voltaire's back through the night sky, and he was **never short of friends again.**

Grilled Sweet Potatoes

They aren't very nutritious but they taste great! Be sure to buy the orange ones and **not** the white ones.

Peel the potatoes and leave them whole. Then cut them lengthways, about 1 cm thick so they are like tongues, not circles.

Dip the 'tongues' in olive oil, put them on a baking tray and sprinkle on some salt.

Grill them under medium heat for about ten minutes, then turn them over and grill them again.

They are ready when they are soft. They take a lot less time than ordinary potatoes and they taste delicious.

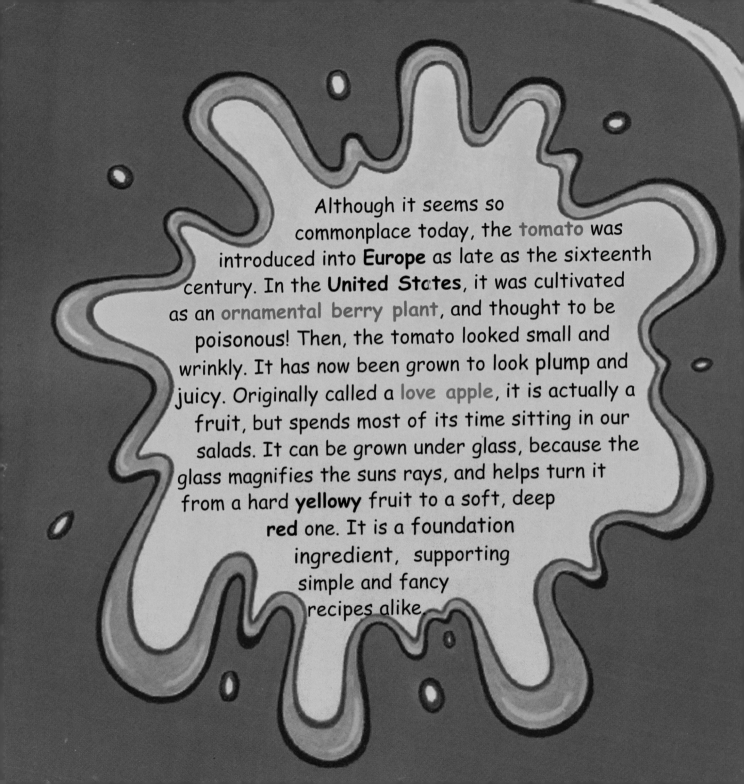

Although it seems so commonplace today, the tomato was introduced into **Europe** as late as the sixteenth century. In the **United States**, it was cultivated as an ornamental berry plant, and thought to be poisonous! Then, the tomato looked small and wrinkly. It has now been grown to look plump and juicy. Originally called a love apple, it is actually a fruit, but spends most of its time sitting in our salads. It can be grown under glass, because the glass magnifies the suns rays, and helps turn it from a hard **yellowy** fruit to a soft, deep **red** one. It is a foundation ingredient, supporting simple and fancy recipes alike.

Chunky Tomato Soup

Put **olive oil** in a wide deep pan and make sure the oil is about 1/2 cm deep. Cut 1 medium sized **onion** into cubes. To do this, peel the onion, then cut it in half. Put each half face down on a board and cut it long ways 3 times and then width ways 3 times.

Fry the onion in the oil on a medium heat while you cut 10 **fresh tomatoes** in the same way as the onions. Add them to the pan. They will sizzle loudly when they join the onions. Now add a teaspoon of **sugar** and a teaspoon of **salt**. This will help break the tomatoes down. Put a lid on, turn the heat **down** to low and wait 15 minutes. Now look. The tomatoes have mushed up and the soup is **thick**. Add a little water if it looks like it could do with being thinner.

Serve and **garnish** with more fresh tomatoes or chopped greenery like **spring onion tops**, **parsley** or basil.

"Rainbow"

✧ *✱ Magic Paste

*✱ Rainbow Pâté

*✱ Hummous

✱ Spiced Rice

✱ Sauerkraut

Every time little Timmy's mother dared to cook mushrooms, their musty, moist, earthy smell would make his face screw up. "Keep those mushrooms away from me," he would cry. He had at least **tried** to eat them... squishy and squeaky beneath his teeth...but his mother said that it could take time to get used to these things. Our taste buds grow up with us and get older and wiser like us. Of course she was right...

'MARINATING'

They call it 'marinating' when you put stuff in liquid to give it flavour. You can use magic paste to marinate lots of things before you cook them, like rice, meats, fish, fruit and vegetables.

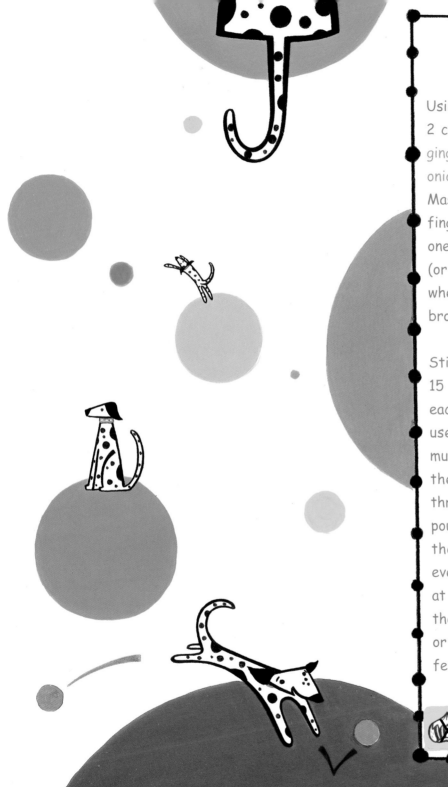

Magic Paste

Using a fine grater grate together 2 cloves of garlic, a piece of root ginger about the same size and an onion no bigger than a tennis ball. Mash them together with your fingers and then add the juice of one orange, a tea-cup of soya sauce (or tamari if you are allergic to wheat) and a heaped teaspoon of brown sugar.

Stir and let the mix sit for at least 15 minutes. Thread 3 mushrooms each onto bamboo skewers, you can use any vegetable pieces but mushrooms are easy to thread and they don't fall apart. Put the threaded skewers flat in a dish and pour the paste over them. Turn them so the paste gets everywhere. Use your hands. Wait at least another 15 minutes and then put them in a hot frying pan or on a hot griddle. Turn them a few times, they are ready to eat!

Not many people know that **bananas don't grow on trees** but on gigantic **herbaceous plants**... The yellow flowers turn into the **banana fruit**. These grow in clusters known as hands and each separate banana is called a finger. Each plant can yield up to fifteen hands; each hand having up to **twenty fingers**. Imagine how many jobs you could do at once with so many digits! Of course, **all these bananas keep the monkeys very busy**...

Rainbow Pâté

Use **cooking oil** to lightly coat the insides of a loaf tin to stop the pâté sticking. Grate 6 cup fulls of **carrot** and add an **egg**. Boil and mash enough **potatoes** to make 6 cup fulls, cool, add a pinch of **salt** and an **egg**. Wash 8-10 **asparagus spears** (whole pieces) or use 6 cups of something else that's green like grated **courgettes** or finely chopped **cabbage**. Along the bottom of the tin place a bit of **green** as decoration. Press in the grated carrots. Then lay in the green vegetable. Finally add the potato as the final layer. Bake for 40 minutes in a medium oven. Let it cool then slide a knife around the edges between the pâté and the tin. Put a plate over the tin, turn it and the tin over together in one action. The pâté will fall out on to the plate. When you slice it like bread, you will see orange, green and white layers. You can use many different ingredients and colours to make the layers. As long as you use an egg to hold it all together you will have some good fun creating these pâtés and they always look very impressive!

Cornelius the chameleon was the laziest lizard in the jungle. He laid on his scaly back all day, warming his cold, freckled belly. He let the monkeys fetch all his food and pour water down his gurgling throat. Once a year, all the jungle animals would go down to the creek together for a holiday, and drink tropical fruit cocktails and play a bit of volleyball. When the day came, Cornelius did not stir. The animals all crowded round the bottom of his tree, peeping at his scrawny legs dangling high above. "Not coming, Cornelius?" they all chorused. "Oh no, thank you. I feel like staying here today." The elephants harrumphed and tromped off. The monkeys chattered and swung away. The parrots cawed in disapproval and swooped into the distance.

Hummous

Chick peas are sometimes also called **garbanzo beans**. Use tinned **chick peas**, or cook them from dried (see page 79).

Mash together with your hands 2 cups of chick peas, 1/2 a cup crushed **sesame seeds**, or sesame **paste**, also called **tahini**, and add 1 big clove of grated fresh **garlic**, the juice of 1 **lemon**, a bunch of torn up **parsley** and a pinch of **salt** and **pepper**. **Hummous** is best left over night for the flavours to mingle. Then use the hummous like any other spread or dip.

Machine made hummous is usually smooth, but this hand made version has much more texture. See which you like better, and remember, cooking for yourself means you can always add more of the things you like, and put in less of those you don't like!

You are in charge!

103

Cornelius sighed.
"Ah. Peace and quiet." However, he was soon hungry. And there was no one to bring him any food. His tummy rumbled so that the branch began to shake.

As he grew thirsty, his exceedingly long tongue lolled from his mouth and rested upon a fruit below. His tastebuds began to tingle. Cornelius opened his eyes wide in wonder. His tongue could taste scotch porridge and English tea. "Mmm. Breakfast." And he turned a warm brown. He slept happily until his belly woke him again.

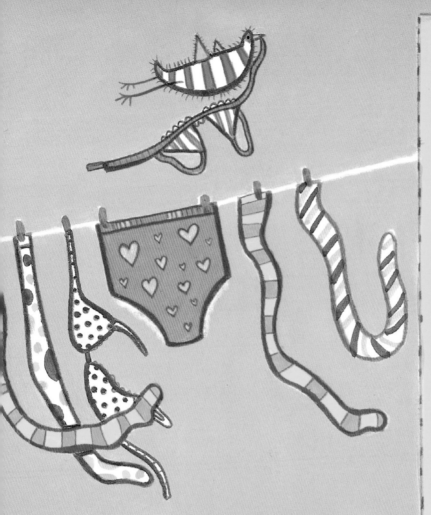

Spiced Rice

Choose a heavy pan with a good lid and gently fry some whole spices in enough oil to cover the bottom.

Use a cinnamon quill broken into small pieces, 2 whole cloves, 2 green and 2 black cardamoms, 6 whole peppercorns and a teaspoon of mustard seeds. Add some chopped onion and garlic and ginger if you like.

After a minute or two add 2 cups full of Basmati rice and stir fry that for a minute. Then add 4 cups of water, let it boil, turn down the heat low, put on the lid tight and go away for 15 minutes. Come back and check it, it will be nearly ready. Give it a stir, turn off the heat and leave it another 10 minutes. Now it is perfect!

Warn everyone about the whole spices!

105

Cornelius stuck out his tongue and looped it around a branch to find a different fruit. It tasted of scones and apricot jam. "Mmm. Elevenses." And he turned orange with delicate purple spots. That lunchtime, he found a fruit that tasted like Sunday roast, and by the evening, he had sampled so many magical fruits that he had changed through all the colours of the rainbow. Only when Cornelius's tongue found the cool, minty flavour of toothpaste, and his belly flashed in red and white stripes, did he realise it must be time for bed. Sure enough, the animals were returning from the creek, balancing their tired little ones on their backs. "Had a dull day, Cornelius?" laughed a large passing baboon. "Not at all, thank you. I've been exploring hard all day. Now if you don't mind, I'm pooped." And Cornelius laid on his scaly back and burped loudly.

Sauerkraut

This idea came from northern Europe where, years ago, there was no refrigeration, or tin factories. With plenty of **cabbage**, people thought hard about how they could store food from one season to the next. The common preserving methods in use were based either on **salt**, **sugar**, or **vinegar**. **Sauerkraut** uses them all!

For this fast method slice a cabbage really thinly. Take your time. Put it in a big bowl and add a cup full of salt. Toss the cabbage in the salt and leave it overnight or for a good 10 hours. Then have a peep. Loads of water will have seeped out. Throw the water away and dry the **cabbage** on a clean towel. Then squash the **cabbage** into jars. Pour on a mix of 1/4 cup of sugar, 1/4 cup of salt, 1/2 litre of white wine vinegar, 6 **black peppercorns**, a stick of cinnamon and a tablespoon of mustard seeds. Leave it for three days and then serve it as a side dish with a main meal.

The Hand series

take our hand...
...into food

food books that are as much about
approach as they are about
recipes...

...with new titles coming in 2004

Hand on Heart
a dead ordinary cookbook
low sodium and low fat foods...

Hand over Fist
conciliation dinners
menus to mend fences...

Hand to Mouth -

no ordinary cookbook

Chávez, Sharman & Stainsby
ISBN   0-9543247-0-6
Price   £14.95 - 120 pages
plus p&p £2.50 UK and Europe
              £5.50 worldwide

Publication   September 2002

Full colour throughout, this book divides the recipes not by starter, mains or desserts but by their colour. Behind the easy to make and wonderfully delicious recipes there are the stories, each one giving a vignette on the lives of cooks and their diners. Easy to find your page by the copper-weighted book ribbon, the book is ideal for vegetarians and vegans with many gluten free recipes and an easy to follow index.

"...This book will serve those best who understand how cooking works and will build brilliantly on what you already know. The beginners will just have to let its gentle magic seep into their souls..." - **Miranda Castro, author of both the Complete Homeopathy Handbook and Homeopathy for Mother and Baby**

"...Is it just another designer book for the coffee table?...No, Hand To Mouth bears the sub-title No Ordinary Cookbook, and to prove the point, there are no glamorous celebrity portraits, no fashion-photography shots of impossible concoctions, no irritatingly hard-to-find ingredients..." - **Charles Hutchinson, York Evening Press**

"...Each page is a feast for all the senses... it's vignettes delight and the recipes are deceptively inspirational. I found myself the day after this book arrived, playing in my kitchen, being creative with old, farmiliar ingredients in new and delicious ways..." - **Nora Cleeve, Scottish Sunday Post**

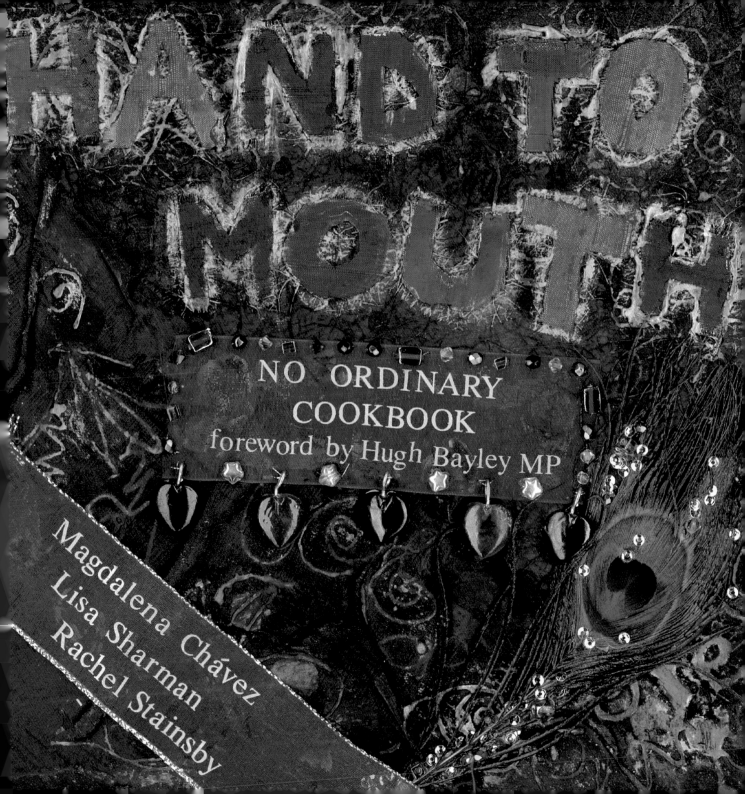

novels of the
spirit

...of what is the
spirit made...?

Novels of the Spirit are an **ENDpapers** speciality

As with any quality novel they have a good story, good use of language and character with depth. But that's not all. Novels of the Spirit also engage with the question, 'of what is the spirit made?'

For the modern seeker of whatever spiritual persuasion these novels sit alongside all those books on tarot, on self-improvement, on life, the universe and everything...

Festival of Angels

Writer	M Sikking Chávez
Editor	Simon Gwynn
Cover Artist	Rachel Stainsby
Endpapers	Simon Micklethwaite
ISBN	0-9543247-1-4
Price	£6.99 - 403 pages
P&P EU	£2.50
Worldwide	£5.00
Publication	November 2002

The first of the York Trilogy, Festival of Angels opens with the two day ice festival next to York Minster in The Quarter

On the surface in **Realtime** all is very festive, yet breathing through the ancient streets in **Angeltime** there is a whiff of something else... Alcuin, ancient son of York has plugged into the abrasive Carmen Romero, who is asking some tricky questions about drugs and alcohol. Local police officer Jack Fisher isn't too keen on giving answers, since he has a few demons of his own. Nor is sound engineer Johnny Wing making life easier for either of them.

As the intrigue widens and Jack's own child goes missing, the layers of their lives become more and more entangled. The past and **Angeltime** finally push each of them to side with the angels.

"I haven't enjoyed a book so much since I read Captain Correlli's Mandolin."
Patricia Neal - Derby

"I loved Festival of Angels. It reminded me of Keri Hulme's The Bone People..."
Morgan Ladd - Washington DC

"... you can almost believe that in The Quarter angels do lean on wheelie bins and watch the tourists go by"
Karen Maitland - review in Dream Catcher

www.festivalofangels.com

In the Smoke of the Sagebrush

Writer	M Sikking Chávez
Editor	Simon Gwynn
Cover Artist	Sooz Belnavis
Endpapers	Ian Emberson
ISBN	0-9513247-3-0
Price	£6.99 - 300 pages
P&P EU	£2.50
Worldwide	£5.00
Publication	November 2003

Somewhere between smoke and flame there lies a truth about grief, where it takes us, and who we are when we come back...

Young widow Em Hammond believes in nothing. At least that's what she says. Yet when both bored and distracted by grief she comes across an article about a boy arsonist in England in the 1950s it sets her thinking.

With plenty of money and nothing much to do, Em sets off from her home in North Carolina to find out about the doctors treating an increasing number of children who are both bereaved and arsonists.

Her journey takes her to Southwold in England, to Kansas City in the American mid-west, to the Big Bear Mountains in California and finally back to England.

But as she becomes more and more caught up in the lives of the children and their doctor, ultimately the journey takes her back to herself. At last she begins to understand belief, what it brings, what it exacts and where it belongs.

"...against the backdrop of sea and mountains, Chávez lays bare all the machinations of loss and sadness in a modern world... The children alone are extraordinary and Em's process is both painful and familiar, shot full with hope."
M Jackson - West Yorkshire

www.inthesmokeofthesagebrush.com

Fishergate Primary School

cup cakes

paper